World Markets

Standard Measurement

Sara A. Johnson

Publishing Credits

Dona Herweck Rice, *Editor-in-Chief*; Lee Aucoin, *Creative Director*; Don Tran, *Print Production Manager*; Jamey Acosta, *Associate Editor*; Neri Garcia, *Interior Layout Designer*; Stephanie Reid, *Photo Editor*; Rachelle Cracchiolo, M.A.Ed., *Publisher*

Teacher Created Materials

5301 Oceanus Drive
Huntington Beach, CA 92649-1030
http://www.tcmpub.com

ISBN 978-0-7439-0873-3

©2011 Teacher Created Materials, Inc.
Reprinted 2012

Table of Contents

Going to the Market

People around the world shop at outdoor markets. They can buy things like meat, vegetables, fruit, bread, flowers, and clothes.

It is important for people to know how to **measure** things when they go to the market. Measuring shows how much they will need. It also tells them how much things will cost.

Some things are measured by **length**.
Some things are measured by **weight**.

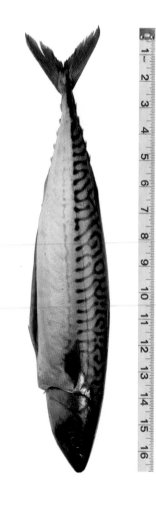

Different items are sold at markets in different countries. This is because people sell things that are **local** to where they live.

Markets in France

Many different foods are sold at markets in France. Many people buy cheese. Cheese comes in large blocks. You can buy small pieces of the block.

Olives are also sold at markets in France. They are sold by weight. In France, weight is measured in kilograms.

LET'S EXPLORE MATH

Other parts of the world weigh things in pounds. How much do these olives weigh?

Many people buy fresh flowers and bread in France, too. Both may be sold by the dozen.

1 dozen = 12 items

People may travel a long way
to bring their goods to markets.
Sometimes they even travel through
the night to get to the market on time.

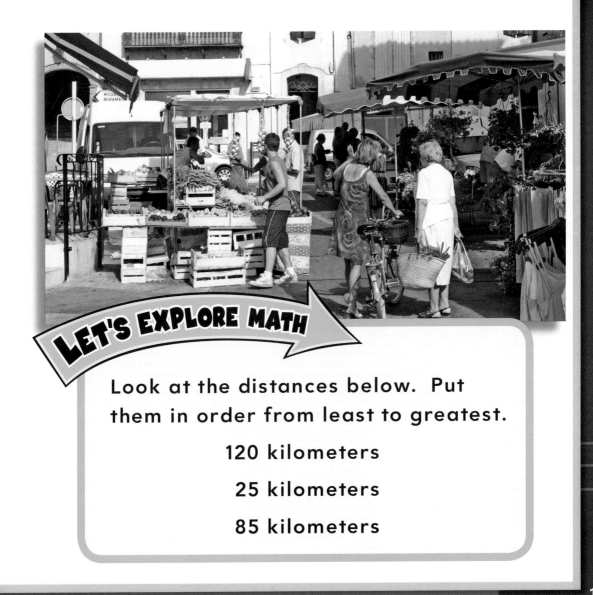

LET'S EXPLORE MATH

Look at the distances below. Put
them in order from least to greatest.

120 kilometers

25 kilometers

85 kilometers

Markets in India

Outdoor markets can be found all over India. Items may be laid out on blankets or in carts. They may also be set up in baskets or bags.

Many people buy fabric at the markets. Most of the fabric is light. This is because it is hot in India. Fabric is sold by length. In India, length is measured in meters.

LET'S EXPLORE MATH

Parts of India get very hot. Read the thermometer to find out how hot it can get in India during the summer.

Many markets also sell spices. You do not need to use a lot of spice in foods. So, spices are sold in small amounts by weight. In India, weight is measured in grams.

LET'S EXPLORE MATH

Spices are measured for a recipe by a tablespoon, a teaspoon, or a part of a teaspoon. Look at these spoons. Then answer the questions.

a. Which sized spoon holds the least amount?

b. Which sized spoon holds the greatest amount?

1 TBSP

1 TSP

1/2 TSP

1/4 TSP

Fruits and vegetables are also sold at markets in India.

Do you see any fruits or vegetables here that you eat at home?

Markets in China

There is a lot of seafood for sale at markets in China. You can buy it fresh. But if you buy dried seafood, it lasts longer.

People cook with a lot of vegetables in China. Green beans and cabbage are some of the vegetables they like.

Rice is also an important food in China. It is sold by weight.

Rice is sold by the kilogram in some countries. In other countries, it is sold by the pound.

Sometimes people cook food in the streets of the markets in China. You can buy this food and eat it right away.

Markets in Peru

In markets all over Peru, you will find garlic, hot peppers, and potatoes. These foods are used in many different dishes.

There are over 2,000 different types of potatoes that grow in Peru!

Fruits and vegetables are also sold in markets around Peru. These items are sold by weight.

LET'S EXPLORE MATH

If you are buying lemons in Peru, which item would you use to measure their weight?

1.   2.   3.   4.

Shoppers use bags tied to their backs to carry the things they buy.

The wool of **alpacas** and **llamas** is also sold in some markets. You can buy some and knit your own hat. Or, you can buy a hat at the market.

LET'S EXPLORE MATH

Yarn is sold in a ball or a loose coil called a **skein**. Yarn is measured by the yard or meter. It takes about 200 yards of yarn to make 1 hat. A skein has 100 yards of yarn. How many skeins are needed to make 1 hat?

Markets in Mexico

Most markets in Mexico sell beans and rice. Those foods are an important part of meals in Mexico.

Parts of Mexico are on the ocean. Markets there sell a lot of fish. Some people sell fish from their boats. Some people bring the fish to the shore and sell it.

Street vendors sell many types of food. There is a lot to eat at the markets in Mexico!

No matter where you go, you can buy great things from markets around the world!

Selling Pumpkins

The Marks kids have 6 pumpkins. They are going to sell them to the Pumpkin Eater Cannery. The Pumpkin Eater Cannery buys pumpkins according to how tall they are. That is the height. This chart shows how much they pay for the pumpkins.

short pumpkins	$1
medium pumpkins	$2
tall pumpkins	$3

The Welch kids have 6 pumpkins, too. They are going to sell them to the Peter Peter Cannery. The Peter Peter Cannery buys pumpkins according to how big around they are. That is their circumference. This chart shows how much they pay for the pumpkins.

small pumpkins	$1
medium pumpkins	$2
large pumpkins	$3

Solve It!

a. How much will the Marks kids earn?

b. How much will the Welch kids earn?

c. How else could the pumpkins be measured?

Use the steps below to help you solve the problems.

Step 1: Look at how tall the pumpkins are. Sort them into short, medium and tall. Look at the chart. Add up what the Marks kids will earn.

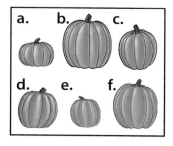

Step 2: Look at how big around the pumpkins are. Sort them into small, medium, and large. Look at the chart. Add up what the Welch kids will earn.

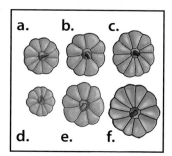

Glossary

alpacas—mammals with long, soft wool

length—how long something is

llamas—mammals related to the camel, with long, soft wool

local—being close to where you live

measure—to find out the height, length, or weight of something

skein—a loose coil of yarn

weight—how heavy something is

Index

Let's Explore Math

Page 9:
2 pounds

Page 11:
25 kilometers; 85 kilometers; 120 kilometers

Page 13:
120°F (48°C)

Page 14:
a. $\frac{1}{4}$ TSP
b. 1 TBSP

Page 21:
1

Page 23:
2 skeins

Solve the Problem

a. $12.00
b. $12.00
c. The pumpkins could be measured by weight.